GOD SPARK

Channeled Messages of Love and
Awakening

Rachel Elizabeth Schaf

BookLeaf
Publishing

India | USA | UK

Dedication

To the seekers, the dreamers, and every soul on the path of awakening:

This book is lovingly dedicated to you, the brave hearts who yearn for truth beyond the veil of the ordinary.

May these channeled messages inspire you to look within, heal old wounds, and rediscover the radiant essence of your true self.

And may they also serve as gentle reminders that love is the most powerful force in the universe, and that each moment offers an opportunity for transformation.

Acknowledgement

To the silent whispers of intuition, the Holy Spirit, the ascended masters, celestial guides, and light of the world:

Thank you for your collective, infinite wisdom!

With deep gratitude, expansive curiosity, and eternal love,

Rachel Elizabeth Schaf, Mamma Bear

Preface

This collection is an exploration and heartfelt expression of my inner understanding—an intimate journey of following my bliss and embracing my soul's essence in its most authentic, intricate, and vulnerable form.

I invite you to break free from limiting beliefs and reclaim the power of love in every facet of life. Whether you're stepping onto a path of personal transformation or seeking to deepen your spiritual practices, know that you are not alone! We're all on this journey together, each of us a luminous thread in the vast tapestry of existence.

As you turn these pages, may you feel the stirrings of your own soul. May you find solace in vulnerability and be inspired to co-create a future grounded in the highest truth: that love is our ultimate power and most profound gift.

Join me in this devastatingly beautiful and boundless dance of life; may we all awaken and return to love in its fullest expression!

I.

Out There

Pink swirls of cotton candy kisses stick
For a sweet moment on the lips.
Your carousel of dreams only spins round'
In this merry twisted-up town.
A carnival ride that cannot last.
Please, no more clowning—remove the mask.
Stop shooting aimlessly into the breeze,
Let's flow freely among the trees,
and live life as it's meant to be.
Out there, we'll co-create all we need.
Being good stewards of the land, air, and sea.
Wasting not, wanting not—kind and free.
From energies of bondage, fear, and greed.

Out there, Gaia cradles, nurtures, and heals.
Out there, we remember our Creators' seal.
Out there, is right where we belong.
Vibrating our distinctive, creative, soul songs.

II.
Brand New Day

Bluebird songs welcome the break of dawn,
As night shadows fade across the lawn.
Slowly, I awaken with the rising sun.
A brand new day has just begun.

Divine inspiration fills my lungs,
With notes that have yet to be sung.
No time to waste, I set my pace,
And face the day with God's sweet grace.

A grateful heart, a happy start,
My humble hands will play their part.
This earthly home is not my own,
Yet for a while I'm free to roam.

With tender care and a dose of dare,
I create a legacy that's rare.
Each moment a gift, a chance to weave,
A better life for you and me.

III.
Wild Woman

Wild Woman.
Effortless grace combined with pure passion.
She stands from the seat of her soul.
A force of nature, her presence is unmatched.
She creates with ease,
From the seed of her womb.
In Darkness, her seed of faith is sewn.
With every energetic fiber of her being,
It is nourished.

Wild Woman.
Pregnant with dreams she has conceived.
No man nor mind can comprehend
Her mystery, her magnetism.
Her innate ability to transmute
Ancient experience into wisdom.
She is fortified,
She is boundless,
She is bursting with life.

Wild Woman.
She is limitless, she is eternal, she is love.
If only she remembered her heritage.
Can you hear her call?
Will you answer?
It's time to stand from the seat of your soul.
It's time to nourish the seed of creation.
It's time to give birth—to life, to a new life.
Remember.

IV.

Moonlight Swim

We are the fortunate ones,
Experiencing this dance with the divine.
A moonlight swim through vast emotions
Of all humankind.

The path ahead may not be clear
As life's tide ebbs and flows.
We'll stay afloat in gratitude
Whilst the winds of change blow.

Downstream we sail, the current guides,
Through every fork and bend.
Fear creeps in, and doubts arise
When we can't see the end.

So many rivers, not one is the same.
Trust the process, let not your heart dismay.
The water of life and spirit of truth
Will comfort us all the way!

V.

Shift

A shift in perspective may be all it takes
To turn your worst day into one that's great.
Glass half empty or glass half full?
Which will become your golden rule?

A shift in perspective can unbolt doors,
To opportunities you'd have missed before.
Clarity blooms when we forgo expectations,
And let Spirit guide us to a firmer foundation.

A shift in perspective can realign beliefs,
So the victim mentality is forced to leave.
A new story written upon your heart.
Higher learning, spiritual gifts to impart.

A shift in perspective can soothe and heal,
Layer by layer as wounds are revealed.
It's a magickal salve from heaven above,
When we shift from judgment to Love.

VI.

Little Lotus

You are safe,
You are supported,
You are sensual,
You are divine.
You are a beautiful lotus;
Rising from the mud,
Nourished by the rich, dark soil.

Soften into your roots,
Feel how they run deep;
Penetrating through rich wisdom.
Finding their way around rocky blockages;
The lessons that help you grow,
The challenges you overcome,
The life you experience.

Beneath the surface.
Hidden
Beneath the murky waters
Of purification and forgiveness.
You transform,
You trust,
You ascend through the darkness.

You bud,
You blossom,
You bloom,
You open,
You receive, you give.
You're unique essence is released
In the light of the sun.

Float on, dear one,
Float on.
May the world behold your beauty,
Your scent, your radiance,
Your healing balm.
A bridge between heaven and earth,
Your spirit lives on.

VII.
Not Only Human

The tide ebbs and flows
In crashing waves and undertows;
A cyclic song and astonishing hymn,
Of birth, of death and regeneration.

Deep cavernous mysteries unfold in the dark
Beneath our sea of emotional hearts.
Will we dive beyond our fears?
Past the wellspring of collective tears.

Treasure awaits
As ancient wisdom procreates;
A future awakening is our fate.
We're all interconnected, not separate.

Stop drowning in small-minded notions
Swim in the expanse of God's eternal ocean.
Let unconditional Love swallow us whole,
And re-align the paths of our divine souls.

VIII.
Crystal Clear

Tiny crystals flow through my veins
Circulating knowledge that can't be obtained
In school, from history, nor scribes of old.
Nothing compares to wisdom they hold.

Crystal antennae transmit the truth,
And cannot be traced by a scientific sleuth.
In blood, they circulate, cleanse, and heal.
With soul, they dispatch invisible appeals.

Boldly to the throne of Creator, God, Source;
Oneness from whence life force spills forth.
Crystal clear, like a river, it flows,
In through my crown, out the tips of my toes.

It nurtures the imperishable seed
that's eternally imprinted in me;
My inheritance, my sovereignty, my worth.
Re-confirming, even I, was Love before my
birth.

IX.

Inner Calling

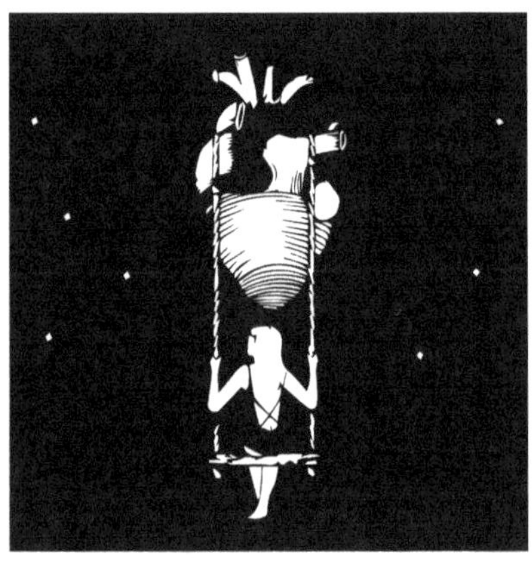

Beneath the chaos lies a deep, dark void.
Beneath the void is an ever-present longing.
A sturdy presence, calling for you to be still.
A divine knowing, yearning for attention.
A continuous summons to alignment.
A clarity of purpose that pulses within
And will not be ignored,
That refuses to be numbed.

Like the hot sun
Burns the fog off the mountains at midday,
A whisper rises within,
Pleading with you to sit in peace, in silence;
To take notice of the emptiness, the void,
The hole,
The holiness, the Holy of Holies
Who awaits beyond the abyss...

Ready to meet you, to make you whole.
Prepared to rise like a refining fire,
And burn away all fear and confusion.
Willing to help you navigate
The mountain you're climbing.
So you can experience the beautiful,
Breathtaking view...
Your purposeful, soulful life!

X.

One True Vine

There's a counterfeit for all things divine,
Scattered through ages, places, and time.
Just a trick of our subconscious mind.
Keep seeking and you will find
Freedom from shackles that bind.
True love that is not blind,
That leaves no one behind.
Life force that unites humankind.
Pay attention to the signs.
We're all branches of one true vine.

XI.

Signature Frequency

How's your vibration? What's your frequency?
Would you care to dance with me?
Who's plucking your strings?
What's making you sing?
Where did that big smile come from?
Wait, stay for a minute, please don't run!

How's your vibration? What's your frequency?
Please leave me alone, have some decency.
It's none of your business, don't you mind?
A programmed response, not the natural kind.
I'll push you away when I want you to stay,
And say I'm fine when I'm not okay.

How's your vibration? What's your frequency?
A grateful bug has taken hold of me.
My heart is blooming,
My head is swooning.
I'm happy here all by myself,
This attitude is great for my health.

How's your vibration? What's your frequency?
Do you want to run wild with me?
To thine own self be true, I won't follow you,
But together we can create a song that's new.
Let love inspire, take our resonation higher,
Till we're humming in chorus with angelic
choirs.

XII.

Coat of Many Colors

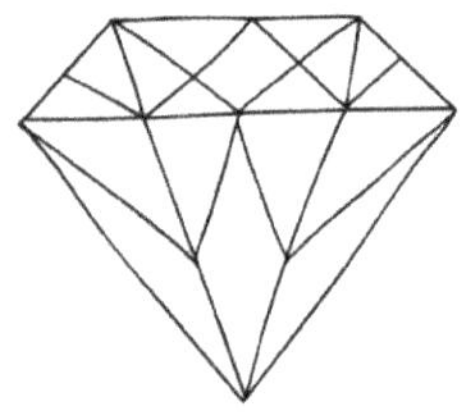

Like a shining diamond,
Multifaceted,
There are many ways to refract your light;
Bend your light,
Magnify your light,
Reflect your light.

Radiant sunbeams dance
Through your aura.
Enlivening you,
Energizing you.
You are strong and beautiful,
From lifetimes of experience.

Hard-pressed.
Cut from a cloth
That is like no other;
Whose threads of magick are woven together,
Like a coat of many colors,
By the hand of God.

Wear your aura with pride.
Threads of light, of energy, of spirit;
Dancing and weaving
To the music.
To the vibrational frequency
Of your soul.

Eternal threads,
Untouched by man.
A shield,
A cover, a cloth, a coat.
An anointing.
Divine protection.

Soak up the sun,
Let your light shine.
May every fractal of your being
Multiply your light
Infinitely.
May our collective coat be a tapestry.

A magnificent continuation of creation.
Glorious!
Whose brilliance honors
Our Creator's intention.
Love,
Made manifest.

XIII.

Love is Funny

Love is a funny thing.
Making me cry, laugh, and sing.
It's the bridge over troubled water,
Like clay in the hands of the potter.
Love is a funny thing.

Love is a funny thing.
It can't be bought with a ring.
Through my heart, it is sewn,
Its DNA is unknown.
Love is a funny thing.

Love is a funny thing.
A salve to remove death's sting.
It melts, molds, and transmutes lead into gold.
It's magick-proclaimed through stories of old.
Love is a funny thing.

Love is a funny thing.
Its steadfast praises spring
From the well of my soul, out of my control,
By its eternal grace, I am made whole.
Love is an endlessly funny thing.

XIV.
My Knight in Shining Armor

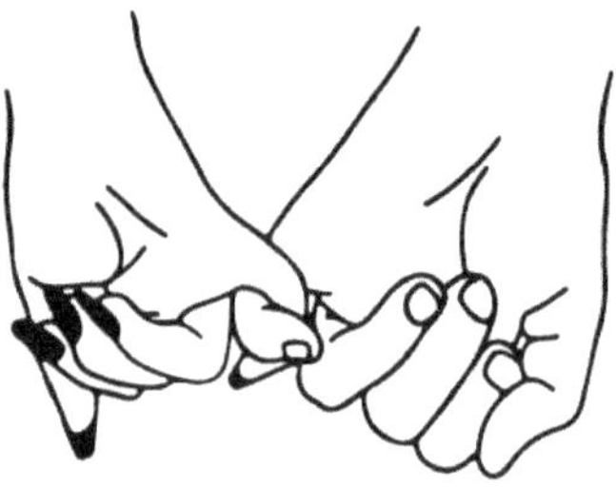

It's been nearly nine years since I laid eyes on you! I had little clue what was about to ensue. Our whirlwind romance swept me off of my feet. Now my heart is forever yours, to keep.

Safe in your arms is where I belong. When we're together, life's like a song; lots of great highs, very few lows, a splendid variety of blended tempos.

Our lovers dance twirls, it dips, it bends; I never want this party to end. My best friend, my husband, my partner in crime. You've become my one and only, till the end of time.

We've countless moments to recall and
treasure. Sweet notes, succulent kisses, secret
intimate pleasures. Your strong gifted hands
can read me like braille. You surprise and
excite me without fail.

You're both the man of my dreams AND the
real deal. A creative genius who can whip up a
meal, fix a car, build a home, craft exceptional
wine, you're loyal and honest, funny, and kind.

Our unbreakable trust is more valuable than
gold. I'm grateful that I have your heart to
hold. It's a devastatingly beautiful life, with
you by my side; the best is yet to come, let's
savor the ride!

XV.

I Am Loved

Summer draws near.
Crickets call in the silent meadow.
In the stillness,
My heart beats,
My body gently sways,
Like the reeds in the breeze by the creek bed.

The sun rises in the distance
from behind the shadowy mountain line.
A new day has dawned.
Morning dew glistens on tall blades of grass.
Cobwebs sparkle like magickal dreams
Woven in darkness, expressed in sunlight.

Birds wake and sing their grateful praises.
The breath of life fills my lungs.
My body, cradled by Mother Earth.
The joy of a miraculous new beginning
Seeps up slowly and steadily,
Through every cell and fiber of my being.

Eternal hope awakens and springs forth.
The miracle of life realized.
This moment is divine.
I am one with the Universe, with my Creator.
I am the vibration of love manifest.
I Am; I am Love; I am loved; Oneness.

XVI.

Inner Child

Magical sunbeams waltz through the air,
Dancing with wishes in the settling breeze.
Making you forget what once caused you pain,
Teaching you how to dance in the rain.
Hold onto those treasured moments in time,
When you were grateful for horses
And the smell of fresh pine.
Barefoot and dirty,
Running through fields,
Playing at the creek bed,
Visions of magickal tree forts in your head.

Slow down, be still, soak it all in.
Like you did as a child.
Sitting in the grass,
Placing buttercups beneath your chin.

XVII.

Separation is the Lie

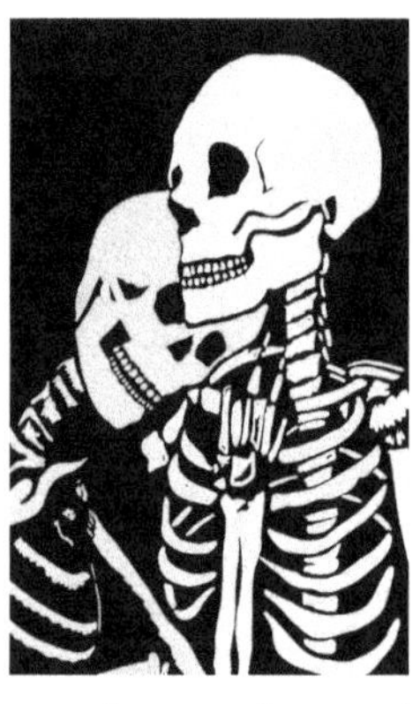

Pay close attention to the souls you meet
Along your winding path;
Strange faces, connections, acquaintances,
And little smiles that last.

Pay attention to words unsaid,
What lingers in the air;
One consciousness belongs to all,
It's DNA we share.

Deeper meanings to be found,
Ancient truths which are so profound,
Our human minds, they confound.
Through pure hearts, they abound.

Each moment a lesson to be learned.
Each breath, a gift that is not earned.
Time is irrelevant; dimensions, and space
Are no limits to what we co-create.

Separation is the lie
That confronts you and I.
Cause and effect, give and take,
We sleep in this bed we all have made.

The illusion is heavy, its shackles bind,
Stealing freedom that is yours and mine.
May the scales be removed from our third eye.
May compassionate hearts re-unite.

The promise of a beautiful kingdom awaits
For those who overcome fear and hate.
Tell your small mind to take a back seat,
Allow your heart and soul to lead the fleet.

No power in earth or the sky above
Can separate us from Christ's love
Dissolve and transmute the bold-faced lie;
Together, as one, in spirit, we rise.

XVIII.

Returning to Love

I am a soul.
I am a spiritual being
Living a human experience.
I am not this shell of flesh and bone.

I am a witness.
One witness in a cloud of witnesses.
I am a dancer;
Energetically experiencing the ebb and flow
of life.

I am breath.
I am the twinkle of an eye.
I am the fullness of joy;
God expressed.
I am not flesh and bone returning to dust.

I am eternal.
I am reborn.
I am spirit.
I am one with my Creator;
I am returning to love.

You are a soul.
You are a spiritual being
Living a human experience.
You are not your shell of flesh and bone.

You are a witness.
One witness in a cloud of witnesses.
You are a dancer;
Energetically experiencing the ebb and flow
of life.

You are breath.
You are the twinkle of an eye.
You are the fullness of joy;
God expressed.

You are not flesh and bone returning to dust.

You are eternal.
You are reborn.
You are spirit.
You are one with your Creator;
You are returning to love.

XIX.

Anointing

Baptized by water, anointed by fire,
Great Holy Spirit, take us higher.
In clarity, hope, faith, and love;
With keys to the kingdom, as above,
So below.
Word made manifest, this I know.
I co-create on this earthly plane
So time will be re-written, again,
Until we awaken, and ascend.
May Christos rise
In you and I;
Through a cloud of witnesses, sun shines.

Let Love fill us like a skin of new wine.
Each day, the present, is ours to behold.
In all that hath breath, God's praises are told.

XX.

Promised Land

Quiet your mind chatter,
Let your heart get to the matter.

Set your ego aside,
Let your soul take it for a ride.

Expand your awareness to things unseen,
Heavenly mysteries, the awakened dream.

The key to free your subconscious mind
Has been with you the whole time.

The Kingdom of God, within you awaits;
Seek, and you will find the narrow gate.

Pearls of wisdom, undefined by man,
Will be unveiled within this Promised Land.

XXI.
The Way

There is a bridge,
A thin veil,
Between the Heavens and Earth.
A firmament
Concealing great mysteries
Which the human mind cannot comprehend.
Which can only be experienced
Through the eye of the soul,
Confirmed by the heart of matter,
Through the kingdom that lies within.
A vast expanse,
Undefined,
Only experienced.

Pure energy.
Life force.
Love.
Love that lifts worldly burdens
To higher vibrations,
To higher dimensions,
To a new Heaven and Earth,
To Oneness,
To the One.
Divine ecstasy.
There is a bridge, a channel,
That returns us all to Love.